I Can Catch Anything

poems by

Ann Chinnis

Finishing Line Press
Georgetown, Kentucky

I Can Catch Anything

Copyright © 2025 by Ann Chinnis
ISBN 979-8-88838-942-3 First Edition
All rights reserved under International and Pan-American Copyright Conventions. No part of this book may be reproduced in any manner whatsoever without written permission from the publisher, except in the case of brief quotations embodied in critical articles and reviews.

ACKNOWLEDGMENTS

The author wishes to thank the editors of the following journals in which these poems first appeared or are forthcoming:

"The Fisherman Talks Tides," *Sledgehammer*
"Snipe Hunting," *Sky Island Journal*
"How to Be a Cowgirl," *Sky Island Journal* and Pushcart Prize XLIX: Best of the Small Presses
"Why I Work the ER on a Saturday Night," *Last Leaves*
"The Cure," *Speckled Trout Review*
"Ode to Home," *Didcot Writers*, Paradise Contest winner
"Professor Curie," *MockingOwl Roost*
"Wetlands," *Atlanta Review*
"The Traps," *Sheila-Na-Gig*
"Time Enough," *The Ekphrastic Review*
"A Confusion of Senses," *Little Patuxent Review*

Deep gratitude for The Writers Studio, which has provided community, support and learning, and for Philip Schultz and my fellow students in Master Class.
Thank you to Michele Herman for your sharp eye and keen ear.

Publisher: Leah Huete de Maines
Editor: Christen Kincaid
Cover Art: Ann Chinnis, 1968 family photo
Author Photo: Carrie Stump, Carrie Michelle Photography
Carriemichellephoto.com
Cover Design: Elizabeth Maines McCleavy

Order online: www.finishinglinepress.com
also available on amazon.com

Author inquiries and mail orders:
Finishing Line Press
PO Box 1626
Georgetown, Kentucky 40324
USA

Contents

The Fisherman Talks Tides 1

Wetlands 2

Elegy 4

Portrait of My Father in the Navy 6

The Fifty-Six-Year-Old Letter 7

One of the Guys 8

My Father and I 10

The Traps 11

How to Be a Cowgirl 12

Why I Work the ER on Saturday Nights 14

Snipe Hunting 16

Hippocratic Oath 18

The Cure 19

Recombinant Dreams 21

Professor Curie 23

Hymn to the Young Doctor 24

My Hands 27

It's a Little World 28

Like Freedom 30

Ode to Home 31

Self-Portrait, 2023 32

Time Enough 33

With love to my dad, who taught me how to tie a fly, and to my Uncle John, who taught me how to knot a suture.
Thanks to both for having faith in my knots.

For Connie

The Fisherman Talks Tides

I learned to fish
   from my father, who had polio.
He'd sit to cast because he couldn't stand,
   flick his left hand out the window
of a fast-moving Buick, right wrist on the wheel,
   and snag a full-bellied bass
one county over.

When I sit on the Withlacoochee River bank
   before the sun burns off the night,
all I need are my lures and the tide.
   Strung out in the grass they look dead,
but when I skim them across the moss,
   the yellowtail jigs and the red-topped twirlers bounce
and I can catch anything:
   a memory floating,
   a glint,
   a ripple widening in the wind.

You may not believe this:
   When my father crossed the international date line
on the USS Little Rock
   right before polio caught him,
he trolled 'round Cape Horn,
   and all the fish turned back their clocks,
all the dorado, all the tarpon,
   because they knew their days were numbered.
The ensigns wrote home: *We are headed*
   to Rio, gorging on mahi. They dated
their postcards tomorrow.
   And the fish swam in reverse
back to their past.
   That's why I sit
while the tide runs.

Wetlands

I am writing this underwater, to be clear,
from a mangle of wetlands, the tangle of marsh
at the foot of the mound where my father built
our home on the Rappahannock River in Virginia,
because wetlands were cheap, and he loved to crab.
You live underwater when you spend all day baiting
traps, trapping crabs, tripping over gills and claws

shaken from trap onto dock, slipping on crab slime.
My summer was one slipup after another, the hoisting
of our haul, my father and his steel pot bubbling,
blue crabs boiling blue, me pitching crabs back
in the creek, crabs skittering to freedom, me
in hot water. I remember my father, his disappointment,
my envy of the crab's sideways flight. Tonight,

it is too blue cold for blue crabs, yet I see
those summers. The splintered dock. The rusted traps.
The tangled rope. My father. The barnacles. The stars.
My father would spin us under the night sky.
Where is Cancer? he would quiz us, each constellation
his catch. *Look at Pisces*, he commanded. At dinner,
my father said a grace that began, *Lord, thank you*

for this meal, which meant this catch, his catch, bless
our catch of the day, catch me if you can, my father
praying with his bait-your-trap-now voice, *There is
a girl here which hath five barley loaves and two crabs,
and the two crabs she divided among all, and they all
did eat—all five thousand.* His prayer caught
on the wooden mallet that cracked open the claws,

the crabs crushed, the hot pot boiling over. When
I think of home, I think of our backyard sinking,
the soil reeking, fish heads floating, my T-shirt
molding, the jellyfish stinging my arms, my father

with his cigar singing, *We are anglers, Annie, anglers,*
my hair stiff with salt water, summers long, winters
lonely, sun like thunder, dock like train tracks that stop
at the water, the creek running fast to the bay.

Elegy
(to my father on my sixty-seventh birthday)

I hated your decoys, the red-breasted
merganser, the blue-winged teal,
the northern pintail you jailed
on your bookshelf. I hated how

you buckled them into our station
wagon on the first day of hunting
season, always on my
Halloween birthday.

You kept softly drying
their rubber and pine,
while forgetting to wish
me Happy Birthday.

I loved to twist a ballpoint pen into the red-
headed canvasback's belly, to biopsy
why you loved it. At eight, I hounded
you to take me hunting.

I wanted to carry
your lesser white whistling.
I wanted you to look up at the sky,
to say it was the blue of my eyes.

I wanted you to put the top down
on the Cadillac convertible you spray-
painted green and concealed
in the cornfield. I wanted to lie down

in the back seat. I wanted you
to cover me with straw.
I wanted to be
one of your decoys.

I didn't intend to slip on the muck.
I never wanted to fall in the river
with your lesser white whistling.
I hugged your decoy

as if it were drowning;
like a mother or father, I never let go.
You threw the car keys at me, told me
 to wait in the car.

But I had been taught
not to sit in wet clothes. I stood
outside until I could
no longer feel

my toes and my fingers. Even now,
on a cold day, when I hear a car lock
click open and inch onto a vinyl seat.
it feels like losing everything.

Portrait of My Father in the Navy

In the cock of his garrison cap—glee.
A young ensign at sea. His eyebrows
arched like an overpass away
from the hog farm, away from the father
who left him. Knotted at the neck
of his khaki shirt, a thin black
tie, its two arms splayed
across his thin torso. One leg
is perched on the hatch of his
battleship, his long fingers cradling
his knee—at ease in a way
I never observed him as my father.

His trousers don't touch
his dark socks, and his shin flesh
looks soft, even boyish, as if the shin
does not understand
all that will follow when the legs
betray him with polio
after his first trip
ashore. A mangy cat is midstride
on the carrier's
deck, and the sky behind him
cloudless. I turn away as he steps
into the skiff that will bear him
to land, this man whose loss I wore
as if it were mine.

The Fifty-Six-Year-Old Letter

Tonight, I found the letter I wrote
when I was ten, left by your second
wife at my front door upon your death,
in a plastic Kroger's bag containing
cufflinks Mom gave you when you
married her, your Navy discharge papers,
and four pages penned on stationery engraved
with my full name, the envelope embossed
with the address of your family,
in case you had forgotten.

I wrote that letter on the TV table of your
Small DC apartment, once the meatloaf
had been cleared. Those four sheets of white,
square paper, my attempt at formal script—
i's dotted with smiley faces—on which I wrote:
*You shouldn't second guess yourself in leaving
us. To doubt yourself is weak. Indecision destins
you to failure, and you must aim for greatness,
because you are my father. You must have
a backbone, commit to our abandonment,
and you will never fail.*

You left your small apartment and moved
home to live with us. I was afraid you returned
from fear of being alone, trading greatness
for safety. When, once again, you left us, I knew
we both were failures—you, a child and not
a father—stealing courage from your daughter,
and me too scared to write: *I want a father.*

One of the Guys

When I was six, my father court-marshalled
me for snitching a piece of licorice
from his sock drawer before dinner and told me
in front of his buddy, a Navy pilot with

eyes like the sky, that he was stripping
me of my commission as his aide-de-camp,
filler of his vodka glass. They sat on
our patio smoking Rum River Crooks.

His friend the pilot asked my father
if he remembered when they crossed
the international date line
on the USS Arkansas, my father

dressed as Poseidon's wife with a mop
for his chignon, hauling a net of wahoo
as his trousseau and how, for that, he
peeled potatoes until the ship reached Rio.

To the mistakes we make, the pilot
toasted, raising his highball. *To the company
we keep, and to the little ensign at our fee*t
Me, an ensign! The girl too shy to speak,

who chose to stand with her face to the wall
in school, my teacher saying—*Ann,
do you need an engraved invitation
to join us?* Despite the pilot's rescue mission

I was despondent over being excluded
from future conversations on October evenings–
heavy with cigars, too tongue-tied to tell
my father how I loved to sit at the driveway's

edge while they talked about the Marquis de Lafayette
and leveraged buyouts, to smell the wet leaves,
and my father's Mennen Skin Bracer, to watch
the full moon float behind clouds. I was ashamed

to tell him I dreamed of discussing things like
aortas and black holes, that now, I would never
be a daughter he would be proud of, a woman
plucking her words from the air like planets,
maybe telling a joke to my father and the pilot,
our three heads thrown back laughing.

My Father and I

are at the Crab Dive on Shore Drive,
celebrating his 80th, the women
at the bar bubbling laughter between
thuds of highballs on pine, and we're
in a booth, four Budweisers under.

The jukebox goes silent and he asks me
how I could be this way, how could I
marry a woman. The waitress slides
over, heaves her cleavage towards my
father's head and recites the Oysters of the Day:

Sea Haven Salts, Back Bay Beauties.
She tells us oysters are bottom dwellers, like
her men, and that it has been a bad year for toxins:
Everything has gone to shit, except filter feeders.
I want to tell my father about how my wife laughs

when I shimmy, cries when my poems
have happy endings, braves hail for a rainbow.
But I am anxious not to inflame him with my
pronouns on his birthday. He has already
turned his attention to the Tabasco. I hand

him a birthday card across our plate of shrimp.
I wanted to be you, I say, as his eyes tail
the waitress.

The Traps
    ~After Rosanna Warren

It's hard to see them in the sun's glare:
crab traps bobbing a line beyond the point,
floats spray-painted red or orange—

a crabber's warning. I have seen
heedless propellor clip a float, watched
nor'easter beat trap and buoy

to opposite shore, mistaken for a swimmer
or bloated fish. I motor under the bridge,
crack the creek's glass, between glare

and glints look for hints of the traps'
path. The water has an algal haze. The current
shakes its bubbled head and mutters. I fished

here as a girl, and now I drift from jellyfish
to jetty. Who was she then, that girl
with fishing rod in left hand, Solzhenitsyn

in the right, snagging flounder, spot, croaker? I
watch her skitter sideways like a crab to deeper
water. She had a tangle of wet hair, fish guts

on her face. She drifted under clouds, sniffed fish
at sunrise. In the moonlight, she put down
her book, shed her clothes, lowered herself softly

into the triangle of light on the creek, wanting
the sensation of becoming someone else. It felt
like joy to be unnoticed, floating over a canyon,

a river bed tasting of salt and scale, steeped
in sweet shadows of souls drifting home.

How to Be a Cowgirl

First, don't call yourself Cowgirl.
Shove your sockless feet
in the red leather boots from last summer.
Ignore your brother's laughter.
Then go find a pony.
Snake through a break in a fence,
dare the brambles to stop you.
Sing towards the pasture as if you are a siren
and your Ulysses any friendly pony.

Cinch the strap tighter on your red straw
hat for lift-off. Grab a handful
of mane and fling yourself
onto destiny's haunches.

Bow your head to the field before you—
the fescue, big bluestem, dogtooth violet,
grander than any garden in town.
Read your fortune in the galena that glitters
through the Missouri red clay.
Let the Queen Anne's lace reveal
your true fate: its clusters of hundreds
whisper the words to a poem about your future
as a pilot or a doctor or a forest ranger.

Let your holster and cap gun be your courage—
tested at sunset, in thunderstorms, by the bark
of a stray. Lay your face on the neck of your pony
and smell how her sweat is sweeter than
peppermint in your Christmas stocking. Notice
how the clomp of her hooves on limestone
has more purpose than most people you know.

To cross a meadow like this is to ride with
Unbridled ambition, like a hive of bees. Back home
on the porch, you would stare at the train tracks,
counting the minutes till the 10 p.m. from St. Louie
rattles your glass with its whistle.

Before you, watch the sycamore peeling bark
that's too tight for its stretch. Above you,
be humbled by the sapphire sky with no limits.
Below you, relax into the sway of the pony. Believe
that your pony knows where, one day, you'll be going.

Why I Work the ER on Saturday Nights
(for my Uncle John)

I learned to suture
from Uncle John, who had one
good eye that he'd close,
loop a nylon thread 'round
a Missouri dirt road, and
throw a hitch that made
tissue sing *Sweet Baby Jesus,
bring me on home.* Gashed flesh
limped in from Joplin, hernias
from Galena, a split lip
from Springfield. He'd close
his good eye. The injured
always left whole.

On a Saturday night, I draw
the short tongue depressor to fix the knife
fight's loser. All I need are my fingers
and thread. I turn the lights low,
close one eye, listen to the fascia
chant to its muscle, smell where
the Cupid's bow longs for the lip,
feel the chin's cleft, bereft for its jaw.
With my needle I can make anything better
than new: a drooping spirit,
a yawn, the sun's orange rising
through the ambulance doors.

This is the truth:
When my Uncle John sat on the banks
of the James River, his buddy
snagged a fat catfish, mauling
its mouth with the barb. My uncle shut
his good eye, plunged his hand
in the bucket, sutured the gape,
and set the fish free. When all the catfish
tumbled down the falls, hit the rocks silly,

they lipsticked their whiskers,
and waved to my uncle,
then plunged in deep silver.
That's why I watch Sunday's sunrise
while other folks sleep

Snipe Hunting

After the cookout, my uncle prepared us
for the hunt of the snipe, which are smoky black
most nights, but under the full moon fluoresce
like quetzals with indigo, their ruby feathers

glinting off chestnuts. Vain with their pastels,
snipes are all ego, scouting for white objects
they live to eclipse: full moons, button mushrooms,
and undershirts drying on clotheslines.

At dinner we practiced the snipe's call,
a rumbling born low in the stomach that belches
into the night. My uncle, a Schlitz in one hand,
knighted us with white pillowcases to bag

our prey, and told us soldiers to take out alone
crossing the train tracks to the cluster of white
hollyhocks where snipes hide. The eldest
cousin, I took off fastest, intent on their capture,

my pillowcase billowing like a Homeric galley,
and me, Ulysses, sprinting through chiggers,
disturbing cicadas with my screeching and burping,
searching the moon's penumbra for wings,

for color. When I reached the tracks, I put my
ear to the ground, my hand to the rail, and looked
towards St. Louis as my uncle had taught me
to do before crossing. I hid in the hollyhock

and listened. I must have been sleeping
when I heard the shrill whistle that my uncle
made when calling a horse. He said the night
was too muggy for snipes; time to cross

the tracks, go home, me holding the bag.
When I work the ER on a Saturday night, I think
about snipes. In every shift, among earaches,
sore throats and headaches, lurks one disease

so rare you have never seen it. You learned
of it once decades ago, perhaps from your uncle,
the doctor, or maybe in med school. It could be
a myth, but if it's real and you miss it, your patient

goes home and will die. On my third cup of coffee,
I remember something my uncle taught me
about sickness: diseases, like snipes, are conceited.
They want you to see them, but just for one wing beat,

so you have to be ready. You lie on the tracks, pretend
you're defeated. Place your cheek on the rail, close
your eyes and be quiet. Before the locomotive's headlight
comes into view, before you hear the engine's three

short whistles, you will feel the vibrations. That's when
you open your pillowcase.

Hippocratic Oath

I would never have been a doctor
if I hadn't commanded my friend
Betty Jean to climb on the basement
table. If I hadn't told her,
You are going to feel worse
before I make you feel better.
If I hadn't pinched the baby fat
above her knee until it welted.
If I had ceased when she pleaded
Stop, now make it better.

When my parents were fighting
and leaving, leaving and fighting,
I learned that soothing feels best
when preceded by suffering.
If I hadn't placed a Band-aid on
Betty Jean's knee, she would
never have hugged me. I'd like
to tell you the promise of softness
led me to medicine. But that isn't
true. That hug, after forty years
in the ER—I'm still trying to earn it.

The Cure
~After Ishion Hutchinson

The angel says find contagion's cure. I find
it in my kitchen, soaking in soap scum and butter.

I discover it in murk and neglect.
I alone. When Lie and Wall Street dress

nurses in scarves and trash bags,
I stand under hospital tents at night and count

falling stars, even my own.
I find a rope and a stick to dance over contagion's

canyon, where ass eating smaller ass look up
with ass in their mouths, startled. The angel

commands find a cure, but make it quick,
and cheap. I discover my cure in Chapters.

That test tube, Chapter One, I call Begin;
I put all life in there.

I put Begin to make my cure loved. Next Chapter
I call Greed. I put money-thing's shadows.

I put Greed to make my cure last.
Next Chapter I call Hate. I put races and gods,

prisons and borders. I put Hate to make
my cure strong. The last Chapter I call Fool.

In this tube, I put them all: politicians
who wrote Greed and Hate, the fools

who gave them a scarf instead of a sword.
I put Fool to make my cure real.

I station my cure's reagents, red and yellow,
next to my bread and coffee.

The yellow radium catalyzes my cure.
I pipette it into tubes that glow like the blood

moon. My tubes will survive all planets.
My tongue glows, and my hands

pulp the red from cherries, beets, raspberries.
My hands, my tongue, my mouth, my cure;

red, ready, a sun rising steady, slow
over a black, soulless sea.

The angel wants to pour the cure herself,
but I alone decant my fluorescing

physic onto the elm's roots in winter's dead,
inhale the sulfur cloud as the tree blooms,

full of green shine. I catch
the apple that fall from its limbs.

I am the mother board, Chernobyl, the yeast,
the bulb. I am all of this.

I take the bite I deserve.

Recombinant Dreams

*A scientist is also a human being who cannot rest
while knowledge rests on the shelf.*
~ Dr. Albert Sabin

Yes. I made the vaccine. My
Polish name is Abram. Iron
my white coat crisply, a reassuring
silhouette communing
with a beaker. Quickly! Stockpile
pipettes. Scavenge sugar cubes.
My library decanters have never known
brandy, only wastewater. My field notes
are from the river Thames, the Nile—no time
for sphinx nor mummy, no eyes for Tower
of London. No Wordsworth or Shelley
on these shelves. When you come upon

pink blush drift roses, don't dally.
You will condemn the blossoms
for your pleasure, while another child—no,
hundreds—snugged in iron gasp to blow out
birthday candles. Our era blooms with
disease and I excel at draft-horsing. Do I recall
the moldy hold of the SS Lapland
when I fled from Bialystok to New York?
I deny nostalgia. The smell of rose water
in my grandmother's bathtub. At night
I dream about recombinants, virus wild
types. My wife strokes my back,
whispering *Albert, but what about joy?*

We live in times of glossy fame stacked
with crackers in grocery store check-out
lines, a life of instant heroes. Science
is a labyrinth. Salk's vaccine, its eleven
deaths, will be replaced by my live virus,

a new shot *du jour.* Heresy will be
enshrined as Truth. As long as there
is polio, my neck is aching while I decant
my pink elixir onto sugar cubes. Can't
you see, my darling,
they are the color of roses?

Professor Curie

Gentlemen, you have fundamentally misunderstood the atom.
—Marie Curie

I am buried in lead. Yes,
my mother called me Manya.
Address me as Professor.
I lived on bread and tea and butter.
There is always a man interested in
the education of his children, at the hand
of his governess. Now grasp
the mixing rod. Now we stir
the boiling mass, pitchblende perfect:
uranium, radium, thorium, polonium,
nuclear hum. Marry for a lab. Decant
the love. He wants to give me a
dress. Let it be practical, impermeable
to the electron's stain, with a pocket
for my vial. The world is decaying.
I am good at counting isotopes.
Do I recall the underground
university where I studied at night? No.
I see atomic structure. We live
in a time of divisions, a nucleus
split down the middle. Fission ignites
chain reaction. Theory begets battlefield
cars with x-rays. My white hair falls
out, my lenses cloud, my bones ache.
It's not old age. It's
the atom seeking stability.

Hymn to the Young Doctor

  Refrain of the ER—your dead never leave you—
no hymn of forgiveness—still haven't written your song,
young doctor—images run through my mind,
a fluorescent chorus of stretchers and decades—
remembrance of sunrises through sliding glass doors.

  24-hour shifts as a young woman working the ER—
cocky, pink-flamingo-socked doctor—Birkinstocked—
unworried about blood on your toenails—textbooks
memorized cover to cover—extra shifts, practice,
more practice—your self-assurance a trick of performance.

  Eternal nights in the ER—your white coat
stained with yesterday's coffee—the waiting room angry &
the newborn blue & the woman in the Chevette in preterm
labor & the old man wheezing & EMS transporting a patient
with chest pain & in walks a woman with bloody footprints,
nose bleeding & you are the only doctor on duty—

  Alive in the chaos, feeling needed, haven't eaten
for 24 hours—what is a day but the simple rotation of two
objects with mass—your ego's addiction to a myth of heroic.

  Reluctant days off—floating in your skiff on the river
fishing, reading slick medical journals—
I must cure mankind!—asleep, your head on the oarlock,
grateful for the metal's comfort.

  Holidays celebrated in the ER—early morning before
the crush of patients—dry scrambled eggs with greasy bacon
& the nurses say Merry Christmas with a Fruit of the Loom
T-shirt—stitched with the diagnoses of every life you saved
& they say you have a radar for who is sick and who isn't—
a mystery.

To you it's no secret—your white coat takes your
shyness away—enter a room full of people, greet them &
you will yourself to feel disease—that's how much
you want to belong.

But you discharged the young mother from the ER—
she had a sore throat & you sat and chatted, she wanted
to be a nurse & she came back to the ER the next day sicker
& when she stopped breathing, you were at home
sleeping & you went to her funeral & you stood by her grave
& you asked God a question–which you no longer remember.

Only to have heard no answer.
Only to have flung your stethoscope into the river.
Only to have fled to a small island where no one knew
of your betrayal—because that is how you understood
your patient's death—you never learned in medical school
where you stopped and God started.
Only to have lived—
with your hands of loneliness dragging driftwood home—
with your hands of self-loathing cooking barracuda
over a fire—with your hands of failure building an altar
to lost. Only to have held up your hands to the moonlight
and turned them like ghosts.

Glory be, young doctor, to your hands of death
that you cannot forget. Rejoice in thinking you are gifted
with a power of healing. Alleluia to absolutely denying
yourself comfort—believing medicine is all you require
to satisfy you. I exalt you, young doctor!

Praise to you for regarding your hardships
as sacraments—it prepared me to wait for love. Behold
your devotion to your patients—it made me a warrior.
Praise to your sadness, young doctor—it taught me
how to laugh in my sorrow. Praise to your pain
that crushed you. I will never be blind to suffering.

Behold your struggle with self-forgiveness. I still battle
doubt. Praise to your courage—you returned from the island
to work again in the ER. You gave the woman
another forty years to do what she loved.

Glory be to the young doctor, the seeker, the healer, to me.
As it was in the beginning, is now, and ever shall be. Amen.

My Hands

The oleander here is too determined,
asserting purple on this sun and dust
island where I am hiding
because my patient died. I am digging
a hole in the sand. I am teaching myself
abandon. I do not care for the oleander's
bluster. I have flung my stethoscope
and my white coat into the sea. I am drowned
by disease, my Gray's Anatomy a brick
around my neck. With my hands and this sand,
I scrub myself bare
of my promise to be flawless.

I didn't plant the oleander. I don't like
purple. I hear the oleander in my sleep
as it creeps up another step of my porch.
Its aggression offends me. It seduces
me: its smell of sun and dust and sutures.
Its thorny certainty chides me. I want
to lie in the hole that I am digging,
to cover myself
with seaweed, and recede.
I want the joy of small choices:
How deep shall I dig my hole?
Shall I walk west or east?

Before the oleander bloomed into scolding,
night and day didn't blame me for hiding.
Now, the oleander is loud
and showy. It is invasive. I must cut it back
before it thrusts purple upon me. Its buds
are soft and damp, like a sapling,
and call me back home now, to a joy
as forgotten as healing.

It's a Little World

as globes go.
I have one on my desk, and it is not as big
as a Valencia orange, made of gemstones,
a pick-me-up gift from my wife during
the pandemic, when I cried *my world
is so small!* Africa, by far the largest,
gleaming alabaster, the Seven Seas
in turquoise, Antarctica
flat to keep my world from rolling
to the floor, but does it matter, since Asia
is cracked where I dropped my coffee cup
upon it the morning after my second,
or was it third, vaccine when my shoulder
ached for freedom.

Now my world is bigger,
but my globe is dusty, as it sits before
a window screen where a dead spider
dangles, its web unbelievably persistent,
if a bit diminished from when first
I stared and stared as we sheltered in place
those years past, my pen in hand while I tried
to write about
nurses with no masks, patients
with no ventilators, and how I was not there

to help them—me conveniently, though
not recently, retired, my stethoscope dusty,
our smallest customs—name it, a hug,
a handshake, graduation—dead, though death
is different now, visible, and day is different
too, more insistent. Those days
I sat and stared while there
was light enough, and I was waiting
to see if the spider's nest would survive the rain,
and if I could write,

and if I, unlike the spider, could live through this,
and how the spider's death felt to the nest,
and if my globe was immortal.

Like Freedom

You can't flick the syringe,
said the trainer, as she showed
us how to tap the plastic vaccine syringes
with our index fingers, softly,
like when people thrum the hymn book
during a long sermon. We gently coaxed
bubbles from the sides of the syringe.
I wanted to set something free.
Remember air can kill you,
she went on. *People think air is a good
thing. Not in a syringe.*

Before us, the line snaked
around the convention center, patients
hoping to reclaim their freedom
while policing how we nudge
the air, without ruining their vaccine.

In my daydream it's not now, it's before.
I float to the moon in a plexiglass orb,
packed with people, laughing, guffawing
the same air, with fear as absent
as the newborn's understanding of the hourglass.

These bubbles in this syringe are more
like liberation, a tumbling into freedom,
the way I recall freedom from before.
Liberation is more stumbling and less certain.

But it's freedom that makes us forget
the sweetness of liberation.
You getting those bubbles out? she asked,
as she looked at my syringe,
as a man hauling his oxygen tank
pushed up his sleeve.

Ode to Home

I hopscotched to Montserrat and snitched
mangoes from goats. Floated
in pimiento smoke through Ocho Rios. Slept
on a cardboard box in Belize. Dreamed
of red-eyed frogs in Honduras.
Wove frangipanni 'round my wrist
in Nevis. I clambered up the phosphorescent
cliffs of Cuba. Swigged Haitian anisette,
chanted psalms with waterfalls thrumming
crags below
                    into their image.

I swam with sea shells in my hair, made
my fingers coarse sieves, let time spill
unskeined, telescoped all I knew into
one grain of sand, which the wind stole
as her own. I became a soothsayer
of red skies and high tides. Believed myself
a prophet of my own second coming.
Divined my I Ching on Dominica, denied fate
exists on St. Kitts. I dealt my tarot
in Barbados, read Thoreau under Grand Turk's
full moon. Paced the Caicos salt flats
at midnight and bid the flamingoes
good night. I plunged into a bottomless
asteroid lake in Barbuda. Counted stars falling
like souls in St. Vincent. Howled with monkeys
in Costa Rica. I foraged for a home
among palm fronds, as the rain thrummed my dreams
                    into its own image.

Self-Portrait, 2023

In the forehead's furrows, devotion
to an ancient profession. In the haphazard
eyebrows, a disregard for process, like the chaos
of my ER. In the eyelids, the dense fatigue
of nightshifts, and shrouding—not hiding, but
protective of one who shields her
shyness. In the blue eyes, an invitation
to patient and to stranger to share their
cherished secrets. The mouth, heavy
with mirth, yet quick to fight
for justice, to cry at disease's sorrows.

This face, seen so clearly before me
in the mirror, reflecting my joys of healing
and my sufferings of failure, never with desire
to alter or erase them, but with craving to write
my other selves—should they exist—
besides the healer, or is that the sum
of me? And yet, with wondering,
and sometimes sadness, as my death
is now much closer than my birth,
what must I write, and how,
while there is time?

Time Enough
To Alma Thomas, who exhibited solo at the Whitney at the age of 81

My page is blank again, Miss Thomas.
I anguish over metrics. Are my rhetorics
a bore? Is there madness in my metaphor,
does the rhyme convey my strife? I stare
at the dead spider on my window screen
and grieve: *I'm too damn old to write.*
That's when I see
the pink azalea by my fence, Miss Thomas,
brown sprouts dreaming green.

I never see azaleas, Miss Thomas, that I don't
think of you, wedged between canvas and bed,
broken hip mending, spinning out scarlet strokes
that float across thirteen feet of empty.
One hundred fifty-eight inches
of "Red Azaleas Singing and Dancing Rock and Roll Music"—
you, feeling twenty inside, wanting more time. When
I look at my page again, Miss Thomas, my words
shimmy, pinhole bright light, ignite with ruby, daub
chunky green. I am seeing my pages
as if from the moon: anew, beautiful.

But what about the voice at my desk that says
I am too damn old? That woman
in my poetry workshop who smirked
when she read this, and asked me
what in the world I think I could tell you.
When I turned my back to her
and spoke, Miss Thomas, it was the truth. I said,
Everything.

Ann Chinnis is an emergency physician of 40 years, a leadership coach, and CEO of Matrix Executive Coaching. She was awarded a Pushcart Prize for her poem "How to Be a Cowgirl". Her work has appeared in *The Speckled Trout Review, Drunk Monkeys, Atlanta Review, Crab Creek Review, Sky Island Journal, Sheila-Na-Gig* and *Nostos*, among other publications. Her debut chapbook, *Poppet, My Poppet*, was published by Finishing Line Press. Ann studies in The Writers Studio Master Class with Philip Schultz. She lives with her wife in Virginia Beach, Virginia, where she loves to fish.

www.ingramcontent.com/pod-product-compliance
Lightning Source LLC
Chambersburg PA
CBHW020220090426
42734CB00008B/1150